UNDER the LIGHT of the MOON

A Journal for
Moonflowers
By Katie Daisy

CHRONICLE BOOKS
SAN FRANCISCO

Katie Daisy, a certified moon-lover, is an artist whose paintings capture the essence of living in harmony with nature. She is the author of the *New York Times*–bestselling book *How to Be a Wildflower* and *How to Be a Moonflower*, also available from Chronicle Books. Katie lives and works in the countryside near Bend, Oregon.

See the full range of *How to Be a Moonflower* book and stationery products at www.chroniclebooks.com.

ISBN 978-1-7972-0192-4

MIX
Paper from responsible sources
FSC™ C136333
FSC
www.fsc.org

Manufactured in China.

10 9 8 7 6 5 4 3 2 1

Chronicle Books publishes distinctive books and gifts. From award-winning children's titles, bestselling cookbooks, and eclectic pop culture to acclaimed works of art and design, stationery, and journals, we craft publishing that's instantly recognizable for its spirit and creativity. Enjoy our publishing and become part of our community at www.chroniclebooks.com.

Special quantity discounts are available to corporations and other organizations. Contact our premiums department at corporatesales@chroniclebooks.com or at 1-800-759-0190.

Chronicle Books LLC
680 Second Street
San Francisco, California 94107
www.chroniclebooks.com

know these
CONSTELLATIONS

Cassiopeia

Canc

Lyra

Hercules

Ursa Major